THE COLD WATER SURVIVAL HANDBOOK

2nd Edition

THE COLD WATER SURVIVAL HANDBOOK

2nd Edition

John Sabella & Associates, Inc.

Cover photo: Disaster drill staged during the Expo 86 World's Fair in Vancouver, Canada.

Printed and bound by Frayn Printing Co.
Seattle, Washington

Graphic Design: Constance Bollen

Published by **John Sabella & Associates, Inc.**
Post Office Box 17392
Seattle, Washington 98107

Library of Congress Catalog Card Number: 89-090795

▪ Acknowledgements ▪

Paul T. Russell
F/V American Eagle
Westward Trawlers
F/V Viking
F/V Half Moon Bay
Willa Scott
Jerry Alto, Alto Video Productions
Christopher Sabella

Special thanks to
Capt. Paul D. Russell (USCG, Ret.)
For his expertise and dedication to the task of saving lives at sea.

▪ Preface ▪

The *Cold Water Survival Handbook* is a set of recommendations designed to assist vessel owners, skippers and crew as they prepare for the hazards posed by cold water. It is not a set of legal requirements, nor is it intended as a set of rigid rules that should be followed precisely in any given circumstance.

Every emergency, every boat or ship and every crew, is different. The ultimate responsibility for safe operation rests with the owner, skipper and crew of the individual vessel. In a crisis at sea, the highest authority is the judgment of a competent skipper on the scene.

Each owner, skipper and crew must adopt their *own* safety practices in a manner that meets legal requirements *and* reflects the specific characteristics of their vessel, region and operating style.

The *Cold Water Survival Handbook* represents a set of general guidelines that can be utilized by vessel personnel in devising their own safety and contingency plans. It does not represent an absolute prescription for coping with any particular hazard or emergency. At sea, there is no substitute for good seamanship, experience and common sense. As in navigation, no single source of information about safety and survival should be trusted as "true."

Even in this electronic age, the experienced navigator uses the "seaman's eye" to scrutinize and question each bit of information he receives about the vessel's position, course and speed. The recommendations made in these pages should be subject to that same scrutiny in each and every case. Some of what appears here may be appropriate for you and your vessel, and some may be entirely inappropriate.

Your safety cannot be guaranteed by use of the information contained in these pages, nor is any warranty of any kind made with respect to the information contained in this publication.

What is certain is that all of the information that follows has been offered in good faith, as a sincere effort to contribute to safety and survival at sea.

▪ Contents ▪

Salmon troller in Southeast Alaska. The idyllic setting masks the hazard of cold water.

▪ Introduction ▪

Cold water is a constant threat to the lives of those who go to sea, or who work or play on cold-water rivers and lakes. Water robs body heat much faster than air of the same temperature, so that exposure to cold water can quickly disable someone who lacks adequate shelter.

The colder the water, the greater the threat, but cold-related hazards like hypothermia exist even in seemingly mild conditions. The human body is at risk any time it is immersed in water capable of causing heat loss to outstrip heat production.

The symptoms of hypothermia begin to appear when the body's core temperature falls from the normal level of 98.6 degrees F. to about 95 degrees. When the core temperature falls below 90 degrees, the victim's life is in serious jeopardy.

Even in the tropical oceans, water temperatures in the mid-80 degree range are considered unusually hot. As mentioned previously, immersion in water causes rapid heat loss. Thus, with prolonged exposure, the cold-water hazard extends to the tropics, while the effects of very cold water in the northern or southern oceans can be disabling in a matter of minutes. That makes the fundamental rule for cold-water survival an obvious one: stay dry. Staying dry is the key to staying warm.

Shelter

Shelter consists of flotation *and* insulation. Your boat or ship is your best shelter in all but extreme circumstances, so there's another rule that almost always applies: stay with the vessel.

Man-overboard accidents and abandon-ship emergencies do happen, however. The cold-water hazard can't be entirely eliminated, even aboard the best-built and best-equipped vessels. That means that those who work or play on cold water have to be prepared to survive the loss of the boat. They may be forced to rely on other forms of shelter until rescue can be accomplished.

Fortunately, modern safety gear and communications systems make your chances of survival today far better than ever before, but even the best gear won't keep you alive if you don't know how to use it. In any cold water emergency, survival depends on a combination of knowledge and equipment.

As we'll see, with sufficient knowledge, even unlikely objects become part of your inventory of survival equipment. Knowledge also helps eliminate the mistakes in judgement that may spell the difference between life and death.

Above all, knowledge helps sustain morale and keeps the mind focused on hope rather than despair. Knowledge supports the will to survive, and strong will is a primary difference between those who make it and those who don't.

Strong Will

Strong will and a positive attitude are more important than size and strength. Many physically imposing individuals have simply given up and died, while less likely survivors have endured incredible ordeals.

The *Cold Water Survival Handbook* is a guide to coping with the threat of cold water. It offers a philosophy of survival, together with guidelines on the equipment and procedures that could save your life.

No handbook can serve as a prescription for dealing with each and every emergency, however. Every incident is different, and those who go to sea must take the information contained in these pages and apply it to their boats, crews, operating styles and geographic areas.

Preparing for the Bering Sea is far different from preparing for the Gulf of Mexico, for example, but the overriding objective is identical. You've got to make sure that the right gear is aboard, that it's properly stowed and serviced, and that everyone knows when, where and how to use it.

The same rules apply whether the vessel is commercial or recreational. The owner, skipper and crew have to prepare for survival before the vessel leaves the dock.

If you haven't prepared in advance, you'll probably make avoidable mistakes in a real emergency. Preparation is usually the difference between a crisis averted and a casualty statistic.

If you're the skipper, you need to be sure that your crew has been trained well enough to help you cope with problems calmly and effectively. In the words of a veteran Bering Sea crab fisherman who survived the loss of his 100-foot boat, an emergency at sea is like a snowball rolling down a hill. It keeps getting bigger. At first, there may be only one or two things wrong and no sense of urgency. A good skipper can cope with those by himself.

If the problems aren't dealt with immediately, however, two problems can turn to four and four can turn to eight. Suddenly it's too big a job for the skipper to handle unless he can count on his crew.

Even a well-trained skipper and crew may not be able to cope in some circumstances. Vessels, large or small, can sink or capsize with terrifying speed. Man-overboard accidents also occur suddenly, without warning, often in dangerous sea conditions or darkness. When the time comes to respond to a cold water emergency, your decisions have to be faster than the snowballing incident, and they have to be the right decisions.

· The Layers ·
of Responsibility

O perating a vessel safely is a shared responsibility.
The owner must provide a seaworthy platform.

The skipper is responsible for all operational decisions, from the moment the lines are cast off until the vessel returns to the dock.

Each crewman must pay constant attention to his own safety, the safety of the others aboard, and the well-being of the vessel. The skipper can't be everywhere at once. The crew must function as his eyes and ears and advise him when potential problems arise.

▪ Preparation ▪

Survival begins before you leave the dock. You can never begin preparing too soon, but waiting too long to prepare, or not preparing at all, can be deadly. Good preparation focuses on three things:

- ■ Equipment
- ■ Personnel
- ■ Procedures

If you haven't anticipated the major emergencies that could impact your vessel and devised step-by-step responses, you're probably not going to do it right the first time in a real crisis. Remember, you may not have time to stop and think, much less read the instructions on the survival gear. Your survival largely

Preparation is the key to survival. A North Pacific Fishing Vessel Owners' Association safety class in Seattle, Washington.

depends on your ability to react with what's in your head at the moment the crisis strikes.

What kind of emergencies do you need to consider?

Man-overboard accidents, abandon-ship emergencies and fire in high hazard areas like engine rooms, galleys and crew quarters are possibilities every vessel needs to prepare for. There may be other hazards that apply to your boat based on the way it's built or what you do with it.

The fact that you as the owner or skipper are prepared isn't enough. Each member of the crew needs a pre-assigned job and place to go in an emergency. Passengers also need a safety orientation. If they're not forearmed, they're likely to make mistakes even if you know what to do. Remember, you can't be everywhere at once. You're going to have to rely on the judgment of others.

Ideally, your planning should begin on paper, include regular inspection and maintenance of equipment, and extend to hands-on practice in drills that involve the entire crew.

Paper planning should include at least a pair of documents.

Station Bill

First is what the military refers to as a Watch, Quarter & Station Bill. While the military version can be highly complex, most civilian operators can make do with a simple "Station Bill" that assigns each member of the crew a job and a place to go in an emergency.

A job can be as simple as grabbing a survival suit, life jacket or fire extinguisher; or as crucial as launching the life raft, making the distress call or rousing others out of their bunks.

For experienced hands, the job determines the place to go, but green crewmen or passengers should be advised of a "safe area," generally on an open deck, where they should muster and await further instructions.

The point is to provide them with foreknowledge that permits them to react instinctively. The alternative to foreknowledge is usually panic.

The station bill should be filled out by the skipper and posted in the galley or some other visible location, and each crewmember should be instructed to memorize the items that pertain to him.

According to the Coast Guard, a Station Bill ought to cover at least the following:

- Closing watertight doors, valves, etc.;
- Equipping survival craft;
- Launching survival craft;
- General preparation of other life-saving appliances;
- Manning of fire parties;
- Special duties in respect to operation of fire-fighting equipment and installations.

If your boat or crew has special needs, your Station Bill should be expanded. The ultimate responsibility for ensuring that your preparation is adequate is yours alone.

FORM D-30-A REV. 7/84

STATION BILL
SIGNALS

FIRE AND EMERGENCY ....One continuous blast of the Ship's Whistle and continuous ringing of General Alarm Bells, simultaneously sounded for not less than 10 seconds.
ABANDON SHIP ....7 Short Blasts and 1 Long Blast of the Whistle and the same signal on the General Alarm Bells.
MAN OVERBOARD ....Hail, and pass the word MAN OVERBOARD to the Bridge. Sound the letter "O" (- - -) several (at least 4) times on the ships whistle followed by the same signal on the general alarm.
DISMISSAL ....From FIRE AND EMERGENCY stations, 3 Short Blasts on the Whistle and 3 Short Rings on the General Alarm Bells.

GENERAL INSTRUCTIONS

1) Each person, upon boarding the vessel, shall familiarize himself with his assigned location, in the event of an emergency.
2) All crew members shall be thoroughly familiar with the duties they are assigned to perform in the event of an emergency.
3) Each person on board shall participate in emergency drills and shall be properly dressed, including a properly donned life preserver.
4) All persons, in addition to crew, shall participate in emergency drills, assisting as directed by either the Chief Mate or Chief Engineer, depending on the area in which they are working.
5) The Chief Mate shall be responsible for the maintenance and readiness of all lifesaving and firefighting appliances and equipment in and around the house, the main deck, and pumproom.
6) The Chief Engineer shall be responsible for the maintenance and readiness of all lifesaving and firefighting appliances and equipment within the engine room spaces and steering gear room.
7) The Chief Mate is in overall charge of the emergency squads if the emergency is outside the engine spaces. The First Assistant Engineer is in overall charge of the emergency squads if the emergency is in the engine spaces.

WHERE WHISTLE SIGNALS ARE USED FOR HANDLING BOATS

LOWER BOATS .... 1 SHORT BLAST ON WHISTLE
STOP LOWERING BOATS .... 2 SHORT BLASTS ON WHISTLE
DISMISSAL FROM BOAT STATIONS .... 3 SHORT BLASTS ON WHISTLE

FIRE AND EMERGENCY INSTRUCTIONS

1) Any person discovering a fire shall notify the bridge by sounding the nearest available alarm and then take any initial actions needed, fighting the fire with available equipment.
2) Upon hearing the fire and emergency signal all air ports, watertight doors, fire doors, scuppers and designated discharges shall be closed and all fans, blowers and ventilating systems shall be stopped. Personnel assigned to these duties shall check to ensure this item is completed.
3) Immediately upon hearing the Fire and Emergency Signal fire pumps are to be started and if appropriate fire hoses led out to the affected area.
4) Upon seeing a "Man Overboard" immediately throw a life ring (with a light attached at night) and notify the bridge by reporting "Man Overboard Port (Starboard) Side." In all cases keep the man in sight.
The officer on watch, with due regard to safety of navigation, should initiate a Williamson turn. All available hands should be put on lookout with at least one man aloft. The Emergency Boat Crew, consisting of all lifeboatmen, shall immediately clear the lee boat for launching. Steward department personnel are to provide blankets at the lifeboat and then prepare the hospital for treating possible cases of exposure.
5) Helmsman and OMU or QMED on watch remain on watch.

FIRE AND EMERGENCY STATIONS				ABANDON SHIP-BOAT STATIONS
NO.	RATING	STBD EMERGENCY SQUAD ( )	BOAT NO. OR LIFERAFT	

NO.	RATING	PORT EMERGENCY SQUAD ( )	BOAT NO. OR LIFERAFT	

Station bills can be as simple or as complex as your needs. This form is by J.P. Grundy Printers, Inc. of Copiaque, NY.

Float Plan

If you've left a Float Plan with a responsible party ashore and your expected radio call or arrival in port is overdue, the Coast Guard has at least some chance of finding you even if you haven't managed to get off a distress call.

Whatever the circumstances, the information on a Float Plan provides the Coast Guard or other response units with insights that are vital to search and rescue efforts. For example, they need to know exactly how many crewmen sailed with the vessel, along with their names, addresses and next of kin.

If a helicopter pilot has picked up survivors who need hospitalization, he's going to be tempted to leave the scene and get them to medical help as soon as possible. Without a clear idea of how many people were involved in the casualty, he may give up the search. If the Float Plan has alerted authorities that there could be more survivors in the water, however, the pilot will keep searching as long as he has enough fuel and the lives of the people he has already rescued aren't in immediate danger.

Voyage and Vessel Information

Date info furnished _____ Type & Name of vessel _____

Planned Itinerary

Depart _____ at _____ for _____ ETA _____
Enroute or Alternate Ports _____ ETA _____ ETD _____
_____ ETA _____ ETD _____
_____ ETA _____ ETD _____
Misc. Info: _____
Purpose of trip _____

Vessel Description

Official Number: _____ Homeport: _____ Length: _____
Beam: _____ Draft: _____ Freeboard: _____
Type of rig: _____ Any hull markings: _____
Colors: Hull: _____ Superstructure: _____ Deck: _____
Owner: _____
Built by: _____ Year: _____ Hull Material: _____
Prominent features: Bowsprit _____ Fish Pulpit _____ Fly Bridge _____
Boat Stowage _____ Other _____
Photo attached: _____

Survival Equipment

Food and water on vessel (in days): _____
Boat: Type _____ Material _____ Length _____
Capacity _____ Color _____ Markings _____
Raft: Type _____ Material _____ How stowed _____
Capacity _____ Color _____ Markings _____
Portable radio: Transmitter? _____ Freqs _____ Signal _____
Auto? _____
Receiver? _____ Remarks _____

EPIRB: Yes / No, Class? (A), (B) or (C). Where stowed? _____
Emergency gear: Flares? _____ Smoke? _____ Mirror? _____
Radar? _____ Reflector? _____ Dye? _____
Water? _____ Rations? _____ Lights? _____
Other? _____
Number, type, color, markings of lifejackets, survival suits, rings, and other flotation gear: _____
_____
_____

Personnel

Operator's qualifications and experience: _____
Number of persons on board: _____
Data on persons on board:

Name	Address	Age	Sex	Citizenship

Remarks

Use the space to record any other desired info: _____
_____
_____

Communications

Frequencies available _____ Call sign _____
Transmitter power _____ Aux Gen _____ Batteries _____
Communications schedule: Will contact: _____
on Freq. _____ at _____.

Will contact _____ on Freq. _____ at _____
Will contact _____ on Freq. _____ at _____
Will contact _____ on Freq. _____ at _____
Names and address of points of contact:
At point of departure: _____
At destination: _____
Others: _____
To whom & by what means will arrival be reported _____

Navigation and Propulsion

Compass? _____ Condition _____ Sextant? _____ Proficiency _____
Radio direction finder? _____ Freq. _____ Range _____
Calibrated? _____ Loran? _____ Radar? _____ Fathometer? _____
Number, type & HP of engines _____
Cruising Speed _____ Range _____ Fuel Capacity _____
If sail, estimated speed under various wind conditions: _____
If sail, type rig _____
Spare sails _____ If auxiliary, when is engine used? _____

Search and Rescue Units

The following people and organizations should be notified as soon as there is reason to believe (because of the lack of communication with or non-appearance of this vessel or any other incident) that the vessel may have been lost or imperiled.

Name   Phone number
US COAST GUARD _____
_____
_____
_____

The Coast Guard conceived the "Float Plan" as the maritime equivalent of a pilot's "Flight Plan". This format was devised for the agency's Voluntary Safety Initiatives Program for commercial fishing vessels.

If they know names and next of kin, the authorities can alert the right families that a loved one is in jeopardy. . . and avoid disturbing the family of a crewman who remained ashore at the last minute.

The more the authorities know about who and what they're looking for, the better they can provide help when it's needed.

The *Cold Water Survival Handbook* contains examples of Station Bills and Float Plans that you can adapt for your use. If you require further advice or assistance with these documents, or with any other aspects of emergency planning, your local Coast Guard unit should be happy to help.

• Equipment Selection, •
Inspection & Maintenance

The obvious first step in selecting equipment is considering the letter of the law. You need to be familiar with the sections of the Code of Federal Regulations that apply to your vessel, and ensure that your equipment inventory meets the legal minimum.

But legal requirements are just that, minimums. The ultimate responsibility for selecting equipment that meets your needs is yours alone and can't be delegated to an external authority. In conceiving and implementing requirements that apply to fleets or classes of vessels, neither Congress nor the Coast Guard had your boat in clear view.

You may have needs that exceed what is addressed by regulation. Often, the laws of morality and common sense are far more extensive than the regulatory code. In other cases, the gear that is required by law and "approved" by the Coast Guard may not be exactly right for your special need. There may be instances in which you have one piece of gear to satisfy the boarding officer, and another to use.

Seattle-based marine safety educator Capt. Paul Russell (USCG Ret.) demonstrates a Type I PFD.

For example, a Type I Personal Flotation Device (PFD) or lifejacket is the *only* kind that will turn an unconscious wearer from a face down to a face up position with any degree of certainty. For this reason, Type I PFDs are required equipment aboard many vessels. There is no question that they would be the best things to have in many emergencies, and yet they're so bulky and uncomfortable that virtually no one wears them routinely on deck.

Flotation

Because no one ever plans on falling overboard, however, the only way to be sure that you'll have flotation when you need it is to wear it all the time. Thus, while you may be legally required to carry a Type I, common sense may dictate that you add a life vest, float coat or deck suit that you'll really wear. Any kind of flotation on your person when you need it is infinitely better than a Type I in stowage.

Aboard the American Eagle, *a 120-foot Bering Sea crabber-trawler, hard hats and life vests are standard operating procedure whenever the vessel's hydraulic fishing gear is in operation. The policy marks a professional crew and an owner who plans to be in business for the long term.*

It's up to you to acquire the knowledge required to select an inventory of gear that meets the requirements of both law and common sense. Some gear, like the equipment pack aboard a Coast Guard-approved inflatable life raft, is assembled for you by a vendor who works in accordance with strict lists of gear approved for ''Ocean Service'' or ''Limited Service.''

Again, however, these lists represent minimums that may not be sufficient for your vessel. If you need maintenance medication, for example, *you* have to make sure it forms part of the extra emergency supplies that go aboard the raft. Two items that would be invaluable in any survival emergency are an EPIRB (electronic position-indicating radio beacon) and a handheld VHF radio. Neither is routinely packed in a life raft, however, so if you expect to have them in an emergency, *you* have to make special provisions for getting them aboard.

Check with the life raft vendor. Items like EPIRBs can be added to approved life raft equipment packs during servicing if the manufacturer includes instructions for testing and re-arming the units in the service manual that accompanies the raft.

You need to study the equipment lists and make sure they meet your needs. For advice, you can consult with vendors and manufacturers or the Coast Guard. Just remember, they won't be around when an emergency strikes your vessel. The responsibility for survival will be in your hands, with the equipment and insight that you've assembled.

Once you've selected your equipment, specifications provided by the manufacturer will advise you about appropriate inspection and maintenance. Maintaining certain types of gear is something you can do yourself. For example, routine maintenance on an "immersion suit" (the "new" Coast Guard term for what was once commonly called a survival suit, then was officially rechristened an exposure suit) consists of inspecting the unit for obvious defects, making sure the inflation pillow holds air and lubricating the zipper with paraffin.

Authorized Facilities

In the case of a life raft, however, inspection and maintenance should *only* be carried out by an authorized servicing facility.

If the piece of gear is approved by the Coast Guard, inspection and maintenance may be subject to special requirements. For example, an approved life raft has to be inspected and repacked every year by a vendor or servicing facility that has letters of authorization from both the manufacturer and the Coast Guard.

Unfortunately, there are "pirate" repackers in operation who merely claim to be authorized. For safety's sake, ask to see the letters.

Coast Guard approval is not a guarantee that the product will work in every case, nor a federal endorsement of certain products as the best ones on the market. What it does mean is that the product has met extensive testing requirements established by the Coast Guard, and that the manufacturer has gone to what often amounts to considerable trouble and expense to win the agency's approval.

As the buyer of an approved device, you get a significant measure of assurance that the product meets appropriate performance and quality standards.

How do you tell if the product is Coast Guard-approved?

Every unit of an approved design has a permanent Coast Guard approval number stamped on it. If the unit doesn't have an approval number, it isn't approved no matter what the salesman tells you.

All else being equal, you should buy approved devices and service them accordingly, whether or not you are under a legal requirement to do so.

Your Challenge

All is not always equal, however. Approved products are typically more expensive than the non-approved variety. If you're not required to carry approved gear and for some reason your choice comes down to buying a non-approved device or nothing at all, buy non-approved. Additionally, Coast Guard approval criteria by no means encompass the full universe of possibility. New products are constantly coming on line, and the Coast Guard can't always keep up with the pace of innovation.

In some cases, there are no "approved" designs suitable for classes of vessels that are not subject to extensive regulation. For example, some boats are too small to carry approved life rafts as they are now defined. As was mentioned earlier, the PFD that is approved for your operation may not be something you'll wear. In that case, supplement it with a non-approved device that suits your needs.

There are devices on the market today capable of meeting virtually every need in the hands of someone who knows how to use them. Your challenge is to acquire the knowledge required to equip your vessel with gear that works.

You want to meet the legal minimums, to be sure. But even more than that, you want to survive.

▪ Practice ▪

The best equipment is only as good as the people using it. Even experienced hands tend to make avoidable, potentially fatal mistakes when they have to use unfamiliar gear under stress. A drill can be as simple as a crew meeting when you ask a series of "What if. . .?" questions, or as elaborate as a military exercise.

The point is to make each crewman familiar with *his* vessel's safety equipment, and with pre-assigned emergency duties that he is capable of performing under pressure.

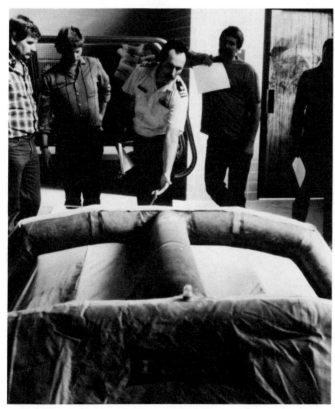

LCDR Brent Whitener (USCG Ret.) discusses the features of a life raft at a North Pacific Fishing Vessel Owners' Association class. This raft has the top canopy fabric cut away to reveal construction techniques.

Ideally, abandon-ship, fire and man-overboard drills should take place at least prior to each substantial voyage or operating season, and whenever a substantial crew change occurs. If you've never practiced using your vessel's safety gear, you're probably not going to get the most out of it when the danger is real.

You should unship the safety and survival gear and walk through the steps entailed in coping with each emergency. Remember, the worst time to try and figure out how to respond to a crisis is when the stakes are life and death. The best time is at the dock, when you're thoroughly calm and collected.

Test Your Gear

If you've got the chance, test your PFDs and immersion suits in the water to make sure they work for you. People float differently, and a PFD that works for one person may not work for someone else. An immersion suit is designed to keep you dry. If yours leaks because of defects or a poor fit, it won't do the job you bought it for.

This kind of gear represents your personal life insurance policy in an emergency, and if the policy's no good, you need to find out about it while there's still time for repair or replacement.

If you have outdated pyrotechnic signaling devices, let the crew practice with them after notifying the Coast Guard of what you intend to do. Consult your fire equipment vendor about staging a demonstration of portable fire ex-

The only sure way to determine how well a PFD is going to work for you is to test it.

tinguishers, and have the vendor walk through the steps required for using your fixed fire-extinguishing system.

Don't activate your EPIRB in a drill. You might mobilize search and rescue units unnecessarily. Nor should you trigger an inflatable life raft on your own because each inflation stresses the fabrics and necessitates a costly repack. You want your life raft to be a recently-serviced virgin the first time you need it for real. Have your vendor or authorized servicing representative demonstrate proper use of the raft when it's serviced. If they aren't willing to stage a demonstration for your crew, find somebody else.

There may be training programs offered in your area by vendors, academic units or the Coast Guard. Take advantage of them. Additionally, there are texts and videotapes that can be factored into your training activities.

Training represents effort and expense, but then, what's your life worth?

▪ The Seven Steps ▪

N o one can tell you exactly how to survive, because every emergency is different, but the Seven Steps provide a framework that should help in any crisis. Later, we'll discuss specific methods of implementing each step.

■ 1 Recognition

Being aware that you're in danger is obviously the first step in coping with an emergency, but your mind may play tricks on you. The proximity of danger becomes routine for anyone who goes to sea, and that's a danger in itself. Whenever danger seems routine, it's easy to forget how serious the consequences of an accident or a mistake in judgment can be.

Your mind may strive to minimize or ignore what your senses have perceived, but you've got to master disbelief. You've got to admit that you're in trouble soon enough to prepare an effective response. Don't let pride or panic keep you from calling for help and breaking out the survival gear.

Preparing early is the key to staying alive.

■ 2 Inventory

What is the source of the danger, what shape is your crew in, and what materials or equipment do you have to help cope with the emergency? You've got to stand back for an instant and evaluate the crisis, instead of rushing blindly into action. If you're prepared, much of your equipment inventory will be ready in advance, and your crew will know their jobs.

As the crisis evolves, you've got to constantly update your inventories. Have the dangers grown or diminished? Are there new hazards that complicate the emergency? Which crewmen are functioning well, and which have been rendered helpless by injury or fear? What materials can be used to augment the survival supplies?

As you'll see, the more you learn about shelter and signals, the more you'll find that unlikely objects can become crucial elements of your equipment inventory.

■ 3 Shelter

Cold is the killer in the northern and southern oceans, and you won't last very long without shelter. Your boat is your best shelter as long as you can safely remain aboard, then immersion suits and inflatable life rafts become your best hopes.

Waiting too long to abandon ship is a mistake that has cost many lives, but so is abandoning too early. Abandonment is the skipper's decision alone, and means that the boat is no longer a safe shelter—that the raft and the suits are now better.

But shelter isn't something to consider only in an emergency. Your every-day deck gear represents a vital form of shelter. You need layers of polypropylene or wool to keep you warm, and waterproof foul-weather gear that protects you from the wind and spray. Without good deck gear, you may get so wet and cold that you're hypothermic even before you become the victim of a man-overboard or abandon-ship emergency. In that condition, the disabling effects of cold water can occur almost immediately.

Good deck gear provides flotation and insulation.

Additionally, you need to incorporate some form of flotation in the deck gear you wear every day. Even if you're unwilling to wear a bulky PFD, there are so many options today—from deck suits to inflatable suspenders—that there is no excuse for not making flotation mandatory for every member of the crew.

In view of the moral, legal and financial consequences of an accident, failing to do so is an inexcusable and potentially very costly mistake.

■ 4 Signals

Rescue depends on alerting someone who can help you. Floating in a life-jacket, you present 2 to 4 square feet of surface area, yet the pilot of a searching aircraft may be trying to find you within an area that measures tens of

A search and rescue demonstration in Vancouver, Canada. The swimmers utilize hand flares to make themselves bigger, brighter and different.

thousands of square miles. Unless you can help the rescue units, your chances may be almost nil.

A signal is anything that makes you *bigger, brighter* or *different* than your surroundings. Your radio is your best signaling device because it makes you enormous and enables you to convey specific details about your location and condition. You should make a distress call as soon as you recognize that a potential emergency exists.

When you lose radio contact, you have to depend on EPIRBs, flares, strobes, flashlights, dyes, mirrors, your voice—anything that attracts attention. Later, we'll see that if you keep the bigger, brighter, different philosophy in mind, surprising objects can become effective signals.

■ 5 Water

You need fresh water to stay alive and to maintain the physical and mental strength necessary for coping with the ordeal of survival. Take as much fresh water as you can, but never drink salt water, alcohol or urine. In cold, harsh regions like Alaska, you should begin drinking rationed quantities of water right away to preserve your strength and your judgment. The grim fact is that rationing for extended survival as you would in the tropics doesn't matter when cold is a much more serious threat than thirst.

■ 6 Food

You need high-energy food to maintain your strength and extend your survival time, but remember: water is more important than food. Don't eat if you don't have water, because digestion robs water from your body. In cold conditions, food is much less important than shelter, but if you do have food and water, begin eating rationed quantities immediately to maintain your strength and your body's ability to generate heat.

■ 7 Play

Emergency gear won't keep you alive if you don't have the will to survive. Play can be a game or a joke—anything that helps maintain your morale and your will power. It's easy to die. You've got to want to live if you plan to be a survivor.

If you're the leader, you have to worry not only about your own morale, but about the morale of the entire crew. Panic or despair can be contagious. The leader has to simultaneously build morale and control panic or despair. The play step is vital for both.

▪ The Distress Call ▪

Making the distress call early provides your best hope of being rescued. Make radio contact as soon as you *think* you have a problem, establish a communications schedule and keep someone else advised about your condition. Then, even if you don't get a Mayday off, the other party will know something is wrong when they don't hear from you.

The initial contact doesn't have to be a full-blown distress call that mobilizes rescue units. Nor does it produce embarrassment or reflect negatively on your seamanship skills. Rather, it merely lets someone else know that you've got a potential problem and you're going to investigate. Be sure to establish a time and frequency for re-establishing contact so you can tell them what you've found and whether you need help.

You can call another vessel or a shore station, including the Coast Guard. Your tax dollars pay Coast Guard personnel to be available whenever you need to talk to them, so don't be self-conscious about calling them early. Even if it's a false alarm, the Coast Guard would much rather cancel an operation in progress than find out about a casualty when it's too late to help.

As soon as you've recognized that a serious emergency exists, make the distress call. Be sure that several members of the crew understand how to operate the radios and make an effective distress call, in case the skipper is disabled or fighting to save the boat.

To make the distress call properly, follow these steps:

1) **Speak slowly, calmly, clearly.** You can only be helped if you can be understood.

2) **Make sure the radio is on.**

3) **Pick the best channel.** VHF Channel 16 and Single Sideband Channel 2182 are the internationally-recognized distress frequencies, but you should use whatever channel provides the best chance of your being heard. For example, in some parts of Alaska, 4125 may be a better bet than 2182. Pick a channel that you know is being monitored, by the Coast Guard, by a nearby vessel, or by a shore station.

4) Press the microphone button and say **Mayday, Mayday, Mayday.** Mayday comes from French words. It means "help me."

5) Give your boat name three times, followed by your call sign: **This is**

Cutlass, Cutlass, Cutlass, WYQ 443. With nothing more than "Mayday" and a name to go on, the Coast Guard can check ownership records, try to determine the vessel's last known whereabouts and attempt to mount a search, but the next item, a position, is crucial to a quick response.

6) **Describe your position.** Use Latitude/Longitude, Loran-C coordinates or range and bearing from a known point. Any member of your crew who stands watch should be able to determine the vessel's position quickly and accurately, and your position should be logged frequently. Lives have been lost because the distress call included a poor position, or no position at all.

7) **State the nature of your distress.** Rescue units need to know what to expect when they reach the scene. Is it a fire, a sinking vessel, a medical emergency?

8) **Describe the number of persons aboard and the nature of any injuries.** Rescue units need to know how many people they are looking for, and what kind of shape they are in. If they've found three bodies, should they go home, or is there a survivor still afloat?

9) **Estimate the present seaworthiness of your boat.** Can you control the emergency, or is abandonment your next step?

10) **Briefly describe your boat.** Give length, color, hull type, masts, other distinguishing features. Rescue units will be able to find you faster if they know what they are looking for.

11) Say, **I will be listening** on Channel 16 or 2182 or some other channel you have chosen.

12) End the message by saying, **This is Cutlass, WYQ 443, over.**

13) If your situation permits, establish a communications schedule and keep your contact aware of your condition.

This handbook includes a sample Distress Communications Form. Make a full-size version, fill it out, post it near your radio, and be sure each member of your crew understands it.

▪ Dress for Survival ▪

Cold is the greatest killer in the cold-water latitudes, and shelter is the key to survival. Adequate shelter must provide *flotation* and *thermal protection*.

The importance of flotation is obvious: you won't survive if you can't breathe. Thermal protection is also crucial, and staying warm depends upon staying dry. Your body loses heat up to 25 times faster in water than in air of the same temperature.

Remember the first rule of survival: stay dry. Don't get into the water if you can avoid it. If you do have to get into the water, get out as soon as you can. If you can't get all the way out, get as much of your body out as possible, especially the critical heat loss areas, the head, neck, armpits, sides and groin.

In terms of heat loss, there is no circumstance in which you are better off in cold water than in air, even if you are exposed to wind and spray.

Clothing

Your clothing represents a vital component of your shelter. You need layers of warm clothing, even if you'll be wearing an immersion suit. Fabrics like wool or polypropylene are far superior to cotton because they don't absorb

The only way to be sure you'll have flotation and insulation when you need it is to wear it all the time.

water. Wear a watch cap to protect your head. Your head is the source of 50 to 70 percent of your body's heat loss.

If you have to enter the water without an immersion suit, the *cold shock* could be disabling or even fatal. Extra clothing and a water proof outer layer like a work suit or foul-weather gear will markedly reduce this shock effect. Extra clothing will prolong your survival time by reducing heat loss, and it won't weigh you down. Quite the opposite, air trapped between the layers of clothing will help keep you afloat if you assume a relaxed, back-floating position with your feet up.

Be sure you have flotation before you enter the water. Without some form of flotation, even good swimmers will have difficulty staying afloat in cold water.

Flotation

Only immersion suits provide sufficient protection for extended survival in cold water, but they are far too cumbersome to work in. They might best be called "abandon-ship suits." They are unquestionably the best wearable abandon-ship devices on the market, but they don't fill the role of providing everyday flotation. For that, you need something else.

If you fall in accidentally, your chances depend largely on two things: how fast your crewmates can turn the boat around and pick you up, and whether or not you are wearing flotation when the accident occurs.

Without flotation in extremely cold water, your ability to tread water or swim is probably measured in minutes. If you're unconscious or injured and unable to help yourself, your survival time is obviously even less. Unfortunately, many people rarely wear Personal Flotation Devices or PFDs—Coast Guard jargon for what everyone else knows as life jackets.

No one ever thinks man-overboard is going to happen to him.

Type I PFD

A Type I PFD is designed to turn you from a face-down to a face-up position in the water even if you're unconscious and in a heavy sea state. Short of an immersion suit, a Type I PFD would be the best garment to have on if you did fall overboard, at least in terms of flotation. It would keep your head out of the water and enable you to assume the Heat Escape Lessening Posture or HELP position to minimize heat loss.

If your operation is typical, however, the Type I PFDs only make it out of stowage to greet the boarding officer when you're subject to a Coast Guard safety inspection. They are simply too bulky and uncomfortable to be worn routinely. There are numerous other flotation devices available on the market, some Coast Guard-approved and some unapproved. There are vest, jacket, coverall and even suspender types that are much less cumbersome than Type I PFDs and are suitable for working in with varying degrees of restrictiveness. Some, like the worksuits that feature wrist and ankle closures and hoods, offer significant thermal protection as well as flotation.

It is simple common sense for crewmen to wear some form of flotation as a routine component of their personal gear, especially in heavy seas, at night or during dangerous operations. For the vessel owner, requiring the crew to wear flotation is a form of insurance against potentially ruinous wrongful-death penalties. With the variety of types and styles available today, it is ridiculous not to wear something.

The Heat Escape Lessening Posture or HELP position is the best way to conserve body heat if help is on the way.

Be aware, however, that everyone floats differently, and a PFD that works for one person may not work for you. Nor does the fact that a device is Coast Guard-approved mean that it's going to do what you bought it for. . . *unless you've tested it in the water and you know it works.*

Fit is Critical

Keep in mind that fit is critical for all PFDs. Too loose a fit and the device may ride up on your torso while your face slips toward the water. Look for a device with small armholes and make sure there is no gap between your shoulder and the shoulder of your PFD when you're floating in the water.

The problem of the PFD riding up on your body can be alleviated with the addition of a crotch strap. Ironically, although a crotch strap does nothing but

A PFD that doesn't fit won't do what you bought it for.

A child's PFD should fit now, not next year.

improve performance, any modification of your PFD voids its Coast Guard approval. It's another example of the occasional discrepancy between regulation and reality.

Fit is especially critical for children. To protect a child, buy a device that fits. Don't buy a big one and attempt to let him or her grow into it. The child needs something that works now, not next year.

Additionally, the more fully the device covers your critical heat-loss areas and reduces the flushing action of cold water against your torso, the more thermal protection it provides. However, no PFD offers good thermal protection. Even full-length deck suits don't compare to immersion suits in terms of preserving body heat. Only an approved immersion suit should be regarded as an effective abandon-ship device for cold and remote conditions.

The information published by manufacturers with respect to the hypothermia protection afforded by their products is based on calm water testing. In the ocean, as the sea state rises, the insulation value of all PFDs degrades rapidly as cold water intrudes and flushes around the body. There simply is nothing else that compares to an immersion suit in terms of conserving body heat, although some PFDs are significantly better than others.

Average-sized people require about 14 pounds of buoyancy to keep their heads and necks out of choppy water. Some require as many as 18 or 19 pounds. A Type I PFD has a minimum of 22 pounds of buoyancy and most have more. The Type I is the only device that will turn you face up with a high degree of certainty. Some of the others will turn you face down if you try to assume the HELP position.

Some PFDs won't allow you to maintain the HELP position. This one turned the wearer face-down in flat calm water.

More is Better

Generally speaking, the more buoyancy the better, especially if it's high on the chest and behind the neck. Lots of buoyancy behind the back tends to roll you over. Ideally, the device should float you face up, feet down, head inclined 20 to 30 degrees back from the vertical. The water level on your chest should be no higher than the armpits, preferably lower. You should be able to maintain the HELP position with only occasional swimming strokes.

Type II PFDs are the horse-collar types, with 15.5-pound minimum buoyancy. In calm water, they turn most people face up, but performance declines rapidly as the sea state mounts. In a two-foot chop, says an expert, "all

Your PFD should float you face-up, with the water level no higher than your armpits.

bets are off." Like Type Is, most people consider them too bulky for routine wear.

The Type III, with a minimum of 15.5 pounds of buoyancy, is the kind most people really use for everyday flotation. Under no circumstances should you depend on a Type III to right you, however, and depending on your body type, the device may turn you face down when you try the HELP position.

The Type III comes in a variety of vest and jacket styles, and the new soft foam models are especially comfortable. Because it is the most wearable of the

This soft PFD by Mustang is very wearable.

standard PFDs, the Type III is the most likely to factor in a man-overboard accident. By the same token, it's a type that ought to be tested in the water. You won't know how it's going to work for you unless you've tried it.

Type IVs are throwable devices, primarily ring buoys, seat cushions and horseshoes. Type Vs are "special purpose" PFDs like worksuits, exposure coveralls and hybrid inflatables.

A hybrid inflatable is a blend of inherently buoyant material and one or more inflation chambers that jointly produce enough buoyancy to bring the device up to the required minimum.

Non-Approved PFDs

There are innumerable non-approved devices, including pure inflatables, some of which are excellent. In general, however, PFDs made of inherently buoyant material like kapok or closed-cell foam are superior to inflatables because they require little maintenance and don't have to be activated by the wearer.

Inflatables are less cumbersome than other types of PFDs, and are more likely to be worn, but are more prone to failure and are of no use to an unconscious victim. An inflatable PFD is much better than nothing, however, assuming it's in functional condition. Some inflatables are automatically inflated rather than inflated by mouth, but the reliability of the auto-inflation system should be examined carefully prior to purchase.

While your vessel is required to carry certain types of PFDs, it's your decision whether or not to wear some type of flotation on a routine basis. Keep in mind that your survival in cold water probably depends on it.

Any PFD should include features required by the Coast Guard on approved models. It should be fitted with retro-reflective material on the shoulder and hood areas. If it's your primary abandon-ship device, it should include a PFD light, preferably a strobe, and a whistle. You should consider attaching personal flares and a personal EPIRB. Mark the device with your name and the name of your vessel.

No matter what kind of vessel you operate, you are required to carry ring buoys or Type IV PFDs that can be thrown to an overboard victim. On many boats, the ring buoys are stowed on the sides of the wheelhouse where they look

Retro-reflective material works even in daylight. This under-exposed photograph of a North Pacific Fishing Vessel Owners' Association class demonstrates its value.

good but aren't immediately available to the deck crew. Common sense dictates that Type IVs be positioned where they're likely to be useful. That generally means in the vicinity of the stern or working deck. At least one should be fitted with a water light and buoyant heaving line. Additionally, orange smokes carried on the bridge or adjacent to the ring buoys make excellent day markers for locating a man overboard.

In the Water

If you fall overboard in cold water, the key to survival is the opposite of the natural tendency to struggle mightily to save yourself. From the standpoint of conserving body heat, the best possible behavior is to remain calm and still. In contrast, struggling or swimming cause maximum heat loss because of the flushing action of cold water against the body's critical heat-loss areas, as well as the expenditure of calories produced by strenuous exercise.

A calm body floats better than a tense one, and controlled breath and pulse rates help minimize heat loss. Of course, remaining calm and controlled may very well be impossible. You've got to do the best you can considering the circumstances.

If you're about to be picked up and have enough flotation to keep your

One key to survival is to try and remain calm. That's only possible with the right kind of gear.

This swimmer is able to maintain the HELP position and signal with the whistle attached to his PFD.

head and neck out of the water, don't swim. In cold water, you won't be able to swim far enough to make a difference in how fast they reach you, and rapid heat loss could be disabling. Assume the Heat Escape Lessening Posture, or HELP position.

Only swim if you have no other choice, or if you're *certain* you can make it to safety.

Use any means you can to get your head, neck and torso out of the water. You're better off atop an overturned hull, even exposed to wind and spray, than you are in the water.

If there are two or more people in the water, huddle together. There will be less heat loss, your morale will be better, and you'll be easier to spot.

▪ Immersion Suits ▪

C oast Guard-approved immersion suits are essential for each crew-member or passenger aboard vessels that operate on cold offshore waters, or in harsh and remote regions. Each suit should be marked with the name of the vessel. If it's your personal suit, mark it with your own name as well. Be sure you practice donning it *before* the vessel goes to sea.

The suit must fit properly and form a tight seal around the face. It must be free of holes or other defects, and have a free-sliding zipper that is lubricated regularly with paraffin.

It should have an inflatable pillow. The pillow helps keep your head and neck out of the water for better thermal protection, and helps eliminate the

A Coast Guard-approved immersion suit is the only wearable product that should be regarded as a primary abandon-ship device for cold water.

The inflation pillow provides extra flotation and helps reduce fatigue.

fatigue of holding your head up. Inflate it every time you inspect the suit to be sure it's still airtight.

Each suit should feature a signal light, preferably a strobe, and a whistle. It should have retro-reflective patches on the head and shoulder areas. You should renew the retro-reflective material whenever it gets worn, with the material applied so that a minimum of 200 square centimeters is visible when you're floating face-up in the water.

If someone is searching for you in the dark, the retro-reflective material will be all that's visible if you don't have flares or a signal light.

Preferably, your suit will include a lifting ring and a buddy cord. It's a good idea to add personal flares either inserted in the pocket or taped to the leg.

Some suits are just big coveralls, like a child's pajamas. Others have boots, detachable gloves, leg zippers and other features. It's up to you to pick one that meets the legal requirements that apply to your vessel, and that works for you. It's got to fit your physique and have the features that meet your needs.

Test Your Suit

At the very least, try your suit on deck. If you can do so safely, test it in the water to make sure it keeps you dry. If your suit is defective or fits poorly, don't go to sea until it has been replaced or repaired.

Ideally, the immersion suits should be stowed in a watertight compartment accessible from the deck, or in an accessible area of the wheelhouse. If that is impossible on your boat because of lack of space, stowing suits in each crewman's bunk is an acceptable compromise *if* they are readily available.

The obvious objective is to have the suits positioned so that the deck crew of a rapidly sinking boat can get them out of stowage and on their persons as fast as possible. Immersion suits are designed so you can put them on in 60 seconds or less but knowing how to get into your suit within a minute may not do you any good if it takes several minutes to get at it. What you want to avoid at all costs is stowing the suits so deep inside the vessel, or in such an inaccessible location, that you can't get them at a moment's notice and reach an open deck.

Enormous Buoyancy

Immersion suits should be donned *only* on open decks, never in interior spaces. The enormous buoyancy and bulkiness of an immersion suit means that you may be trapped if you put it on inside a vessel that rolls suddenly.

Immersion suits should be kept completely dry and stowed in the bag provided by the manufacturer. To eject the suit, simply hold the bag upside down and thrust it sharply downward.

Wear as much clothing as you can under the suit, including a watch cap and shoes or boots. Be sure that you have practiced in advance and are certain that the clothes and boots you intend to wear will fit. Don't waste time struggling to get your boots and deck gear into the suit when it's time to abandon ship. If it comes down to a choice between getting into the suit or keeping your boots and deck gear, get rid of them. Getting the suit on before you enter the water is by far your highest priority.

On a rolling deck, sit down and put the suit on like a child's pajamas. First, get your feet in the legs. Next, put your weak arm in one sleeve. While your strong arm remains free, use it to get the hood over your head. Put your strong arm in its sleeve after the rest of the suit is on.

Arch Your Back

Arch your back to remove wrinkles in the fabric as you zip, and close the face flap before you enter the water.

To zip an immersion suit, find the zipper, then arch your back.

Unless you have a suit with detachable gloves or a zippered hand opening, you will have virtually no use of your hands with the suit on.

To prepare early and still have the use of your hands, put on the lower half of the suit and tie the arms around your waist like a ski sweater. This way, you can make a distress call or continue trying to save the vessel but still be ready to abandon in an instant.

Put on the lower half of the suit and tie the arms around your waist to be ready to abandon while you try to save the boat.

Be sure that your zipper has a lanyard or tail long enough to enable you to grasp it easily with the gloves on.

Use the mouth tube or CO_2 inflator to fill the pillow only after you have entered the water.

Enter the water from the lowest possible point, and look before you leap. You've got to protect yourself from injury, especially if you're very high. Jumping sideways enables you to use your inboard arm to protect your head from striking the vessel in a sudden roll. Cover your face with your other hand to minimize the cold shock. Cross your legs or keep your feet tight together as you hit the water in case there is floating debris.

Peter Rowe of Fitzwright Survival Systems demonstrates good jump technique. His feet are crossed in case there is debris in the water that could cause an injury in jumping from a substantial height. He jumps sideways and uses his inboard arm to protect his head in case the vessel rolls and causes him to strike the hull. His outboard hand protects his face.

Inspection, Stowage

If your suit has been exposed to salt water, rinse it thoroughly with fresh water. Dry it inside out, then turn it rightside out and dry it again. It must be completely dry before you stow it in the bag.

Immersion suits should be inspected frequently. Corroded or malfunctioning zippers should be replaced immediately by the manufacturer or someone qualified to repair dry diving suits. The zipper should be lubricated after each inspection. Look for leaks or rips in the fabric, inspect the stitching and gluing along each seam, and test the inflation pillow and mouth tube. Any defect, no matter how small, is cause for immediate repair or replacement.

Stow the suit so it's ready for immediate use. Deflate the inflation pillow, pull the zipper all the way down and fold the face flap out of the way. Make sure the lifting ring is disconnected and that nothing else could interfere with your ability to put the suit on in a hurry. Begin folding carefully at the feet, pull the hood down and fold the arms across the bundle. Close all snaps on the bag for maximum protection of the suit.

▪ Inflatable Life Rafts ▪

The combination of an immersion suit and inflatable life raft makes your chances of survival today far better than ever before. But merely having the equipment aboard is no guarantee that you'll survive. You need to know how to use it.

Part of your preparation should be to read the instructions provided by the manufacturers of your survival equipment. Try to anticipate the circumstances that you could someday face, and visualize your responses. The more you've thought about survival procedures in advance, and the better you know your equipment, the better the chances you'll put it to its best use in a real emergency.

Abandoning ship is the skipper's decision, no one else's. Just as it's a crucial mistake to wait too long to begin survival procedures, abandoning too

Inflatable life rafts and immersion suits increase your survival chances enormously, but only if you know how to use them. This raft has come out of the cannister upside down and has to be righted.

soon has cost lives unnecessarily. Your boat is your best shelter in all but the most extreme circumstances, and the moment to abandon is the moment when the life raft and the immersion suits represent better shelter than the boat.

Each crewman should understand the operation of the life raft on his vessel, and be aware of the equipment it contains. Many vessels are legally required to carry Coast Guard-approved rafts that are serviced annually by an authorized servicing facility. Even with no legal requirement, if your vessel operates offshore or in cold or remote conditions, you should do the same.

Cannisters, Valise Packs

Rafts come in hard cannisters and valise packs. Currently, the smallest Coast Guard-approved models have four-man capacity. Additionally, there are various types of buoyant apparatus and buoyant skiffs that serve as adequate survival platforms in certain applications. Be sure you select a piece of gear that satisfies the regulations *and* works in the environment where you go to sea.

Brian Hough of Westmar Services, Inc. of Seattle demonstrates a hard-cannister life raft at a North Pacific Fishing Vessel Owners' Association class. Your vendor or authorized servicing representative should be happy to demonstrate the features of your raft to you and your crew. If he isn't, find somebody else.

In practice exercises, don't inflate your raft with the CO_2 cylinder because of stress on the fabric and the cost of repacking. To familiarize yourself and your crew with the operation of your raft, contact your vendor or authorized servicing representative. He should be happy to let you observe as he inflates the raft and inspects the contents.

A hard-cannister raft should be stowed on a cradle in a manner that provides easy access and permits a "float free" launch if the vessel sinks suddenly. It must be stowed clear of rigging or superstructures that could interfere with its ability to float free.

The life raft cannister should be secured to the cradle by a hydrostatic release that is activated by water pressure if the vessel sinks suddenly. There should be no other lashings or tie-downs that restrict the raft from floating free.

For manual launching, release the pelican hook on the raft's tie-down strap, or kick or strike the trigger on the hydrostatic release, and lift the cannister off the cradle. Larger cannisters have handholds at the ends.

Whenever it is handled, the cannister must be treated carefully to prevent punctures and ensure that the watertight gasket remains intact. Carry the cannister upright. Turning the raft upside down could cause the painter to foul and inhibit inflation.

The cannister is held together by metal bands. These bands break automatically during launching.

Attach the Painter

As soon as the cannister is installed in the cradle, the painter should be attached to the vessel structure, and should remain attached *whenever* the vessel is at sea. The painter-to-vessel connection includes a weak link designed to break during a float-free launch.

Try to launch the raft before the emergency reaches the crisis stage. Many vessels stow the raft on the housetop, or in some other out-of-the-way location

These crewmen from the Bering Sea crabber-trawler Half Moon Bay *demonstrate manual launch procedures. The man at the right has pulled a few feet of painter line out of the cannister and is belaying the line to the cleat on the cradle prior to tossing the raft overboard.*

where it doesn't interfere with normal operations. When it's time to abandon ship, however, it's preferable to launch and board the raft from the lowest possible point above the water. You need to strike the best available compromise on your boat between what's convenient in terms of stowage, and what is workable when it's time to launch the life raft.

It may be extremely difficult to reach the stowage area and launch the raft manually in heavy seas. If your raft is stowed atop the house or in some other hard-to-reach location, consider installing toe rails or non-skid around the cradle to provide better footing, and devise a means of lowering the raft to the deck during a controlled abandonment.

If you do attempt to move the raft prior to launching, be sure to maintain firm control over the painter. The full strength of the painter is required when the raft goes into the water. Stated differently, the raft should never be launched unless it is secured to the vessel with the full strength of the painter line.

Painter-to-Vessel

Before launching the raft manually, change the painter-to-vessel connection so that the full strength of the painter line takes the place of the weak link designed only for float free launches. Pull out a few feet of painter line from the cannister and belay it to the cleat located on the raft cradle, or to some other nearby strong point. This bypasses the weak link and ensures that the full strength of the line secures the raft.

The raft should be launched over the lee side, or the wind will pin you to the vessel and create the potential of damage to the raft. Pulling the painter out to its full length activates the inflation. The painter on a Coast Guard-approved raft has traditionally been 100 feet long, although this length standard has been under review and may be revised upward.

Your raft will probably over-inflate and you'll hear air escaping through pressure relief valves.

Wait for full inflation, with the canopy erect, before boarding. Your raft will probably over-inflate, and you'll hear the sound of air escaping through pressure-relief valves. This does not mean that the raft is defective. The sound should cease quickly.

Don't Get Wet

If you can, board the raft directly without getting wet. Staying dry is the first rule of survival. If the distance is short, step or jump directly into the canopy entrance. You may be able to use a ladder, net or line to get yourself close enough to the canopy entrance to board directly.

Raft canopies are designed to withstand the impact of people jumping on them from a height of 15 feet, but only attempt to jump onto the canopy as a last resort. If the height is more than a few feet, jumping onto the canopy may cause injury to you or to someone inside, or may cause you to bounce overboard and wind up in the water.

If you must enter the water, do so as close as possible to the raft and try to hold onto the painter. Without something to hold onto, you could be swept beyond the raft. Above all, think before you jump. Jump from the lowest possible point and beware of hazards below you.

If the raft is inverted, right it by means of the righting strap on the bottom. Right it from the side with the CO_2 cylinder, where it says "Right Here." If you right it from the opposite side, the heavy cylinder may knock you out when the raft turns over.

As you right the raft, it may land on top of you. Don't panic. You can push an airpocket into the soft bottom of the raft if you get your nose close to the fabric. Lie on your back and work your way out hand over hand.

To right an inverted raft, start at the side with the CO_2 cylinder and use the righting strap to pull it over.

Boarding

Boarding the raft from the water can be difficult. You may have to bob down and use the buoyancy of your immersion suit or PFD to enable you to grab the lifelines inside and pull yourself in. Rafts have inflatable boarding ramps or webbed boarding ladders to help you.

Once you're inside, help others get aboard. Use the heaving line stowed near the canopy entrance to help your crewmates reach the raft. You can slip the heaving ring around your arm to create a lifeline if you have to swim to help another crewman.

When you're aboard, help your crewmates.

If you suspect that a crewman has back or neck injuries, handle him as gently as possible.

Don't cut the painter if you don't have to. Your vessel may not sink and you may be able to reboard. If it capsizes without jeopardizing the raft and remains afloat, it will provide a sea anchor that keeps you close to your last reported position, and it makes a better search target than the raft. If it sinks in shallow water, you may be able to use it as an anchor that keeps you at your last reported position.

Safety Knife

If the vessel represents a danger to the raft, cut the painter with the safety knife stowed near the entrance of each Coast Guard-approved raft.

If you operate more than 20 miles offshore, your raft should contain an Ocean Service Pack. For operations within 20 miles, or in lakes, bays and sounds, you can substitute a smaller Limited Service Pack. Before you go to sea, you should be aware of exactly what your raft contains. The equipment packs

Don't cut the painter unless you have to. There's a safety knife at the canopy entrance of each Coast Guard-approved raft you can use if you do have to cut it.

represent a form of inventory that is prepared for you in advance, but you bear the responsibility for ensuring that the equipment aboard your raft meets your needs.

Don't allow yourself to be surprised at what the raft *does not* contain. For example, unless you've made special arrangements with the manufacturer, an approved raft won't contain items like an EPIRB, a hand-held radio or prescription medicine.

If you have time, augment the equipment pack with items from the vessel. Grab the handheld radio, the EPIRB, extra food and water, blankets, clothing. . . whatever you can find.

Try to throw everything that floats over the side just before you abandon. Throw buoys, fenders, planks, coolers, plastic bottles. . . you may have to use them for flotation. In any case, the floating debris represents a signal that makes you bigger and different. If you have time, tie the debris together. If it doesn't represent a potential source of damage, tie it to the raft.

Throw debris over the side if you have time. It provides a source of flotation and represents a signal that makes you bigger, brighter and different.

Inflate the Floor

An approved raft contains a hand pump and you should use it quickly to pump up the raft floor and provide added insulation against the cold. On an approved raft, a drogue or sea anchor should be deployed as the raft inflates. A life raft drifts extremely rapidly, and you want to stay as close as possible to your last reported position.

Check to see if the drogue is working. There is a spare in the equipment pack on approved rafts, although unapproved rafts may have no drogues at all. If you don't have one, try to make one out of a bucket or some other material.

The service pack contains sea sickness pills. Take them, no matter how strong your stomach is. The pitching and rolling of a life raft makes everybody sick.

Establish a chain of command, and set watches. You need a lookout at the canopy entrance, and should assign other crewmen to inspect the raft for damage, to bail or pump out water, to treat injuries and to inventory equipment.

If you're the leader, boosting morale is a critical part of your job. Remember the *play* step, and focus on surviving instead of despair. Displaying the contents of the equipment pack and any other supplies you have been able to bring aboard is a good way to demonstrate that you have resources. Giving people jobs is another way to focus their minds on life, but don't waste their energy.

Don't permit a crewman who has panicked to threaten the group morale.

If there is more than one raft in the water, tie them together. The rafts will ride better in a heavy sea state and be less likely to capsize, you'll have more resources as a group, morale will be easier to maintain and you'll make a bigger search target.

▪ Distress Signals ▪

Rescue depends upon your ability to alert someone who can help you. Remember, your radio is your best signaling device, and you should make a distress call as soon as you think an emergency *may* exist. Your vessel should be equipped with an emergency power supply to provide radio transmission capability despite the loss of the main power system.

In a controlled abandonment, you may be able to bring a hand-held radio aboard the raft. Conserve the batteries by making periodic distress calls with the hand-held until you make contact.

EPIRBs, or emergency position-indicating radio beacons, are vital distress signals. They are electronic transmitters with built-in battery packs that transmit distress signals on international search and rescue frequencies. There have traditionally been three types:

Class A, automatic;
Class B, manual;
Class C, for use within 20 miles offshore.

406 MHz

Specifications for a new type, Category 1 or "Satellite EPIRBs" operating at 406 MHz, were under development in 1988. Once the new units become commercially available, they will make the older types obsolete after a phase-in period determined by the Coast Guard. Consult your local Coast Guard office for the latest information on type requirements for your vessel.

EPIRBs are not included as standard equipment aboard life rafts, although you can have them added to the equipment pack if the raft manufacturer includes instructions for testing and re-arming the units in the raft service manual.

Class A EPIRBs are designed to be installed aboard the vessel in a float-free manner. They will begin emitting signals automatically as soon as they are immersed in water and turned upright. They should not be lashed or secured to the vessel in a way that prevents them from floating free in a sudden capsize.

Class A EPIRBs transmit at 121.5 MHz (the civil aviation distress frequency) and 243 MHz (the military aviation distress frequency).

Class B EPIRBs transmit on the same frequencies and have manual on/off switches.

Class C EPIRBs are manually operated and transmit line-of-sight signals at 156.75 and 156.8 MHz (VHF channels 15 and 16). These units have a maximum transmission range of about 20 miles depending on the height of the antenna. They are of limited use for inshore or near-shore vessel operations.

Whichever type you have, be sure you understand how to activate the unit so you are certain that it's transmitting when you need it.

SARSAT

EPIRB signals from Class A or B units are usually picked up by aircraft or the SARSAT (Search and Rescue Satellite-Aided Tracking) System. Search and rescue satellites operated by the U.S. and the Soviet Union that pick up multiple signals from the older-style EPIRB units are capable of fixing your position within five to 10 miles.

The 406 MHz system reduces that figure to from one to three miles and provides considerably more assurance that you'll be found. While 406 MHz units are going to be more expensive than older-style EPIRBs, at least initially, they facilitate a significantly more accurate, more comprehensive and more dependable SARSAT system.

The ability of rescue units to fix your position depends on a steady EPIRB signal. In an emergency, *turn your EPIRB on and leave it on.* If you have multiple units, use them alternately for periods of six hours each, always maintaining a constant transmission.

The SARSAT system has saved hundreds of lives, but the vast majority of the signals received are false alarms. Don't activate your EPIRB unnecessarily. You may mobilize rescue units that should be responding to a real emergency, and you could be fined.

While anyone can (and should) use an EPIRB in an emergency, you are required to be a licensed radio operator to test the units, and they should be tested *only* for a period of three sweeps (about half a second) during the first five minutes of every hour. Follow the manufacturer's instructions to the letter in testing an EPIRB and renewing the batteries.

Visual Distress Signals

A visual distress signal is anything that makes you bigger, brighter or different.

To make yourself bigger, stay with the boat, tie your rafts together, huddle in a group, collect debris...do whatever circumstances permit. As we discussed in the previous chapter, before you abandon ship, throw everything that floats over the side. The debris may provide emergency flotation, and it makes you bigger and different.

Searchers always investigate debris. One veteran Coast Guard pilot says Clorox bottles have led him to casualties more than once. He once rescued a boy

The brilliant light and smoke produced by hand flares is effective night or day. Modern hand flares come in metal cannisters, with internal triggering mechanisms. They are far superior to the old, highway-type that have to be struck for ignition.

who had floated for days in a Coleman cooler his father had pitched over the side.

By yourself, you make a tiny search target. You've got to help the rescue units.

Pyrotechnic flares and rockets make you bigger and brighter. They're included in Coast Guard-approved life rafts, but any vessel that operates in offshore or remote locations should consider augmenting the quantities in the raft and carrying extras on the bridge.

Additionally, crewmen should consider attaching pyrotechnic signals to their PFDs and immersion suits, or putting them in the Personal Survival Kits we'll discuss later. Like flotation, pyrotechnics are no good if you don't have them with you.

The pyrotechnics available on the market today include the low-intensity "recreational" type—pistol-launched meteors and 500-candlepower hand-flares—and the modern "commercial" variety. If you confront a cold water hazard and want to boost your chances of being seen by rescue units, you should carry commercial-grade pyrotechnics.

Rule of Thumb

A good rule of thumb is to carry at least three 15,000-candlepower hand flares and one 40,000-candlepower parachute rocket on the bridge. Coast Guard-approved life rafts contains six 15,000-candlepower hand flares and three 40,000-candlepower parachute rockets.

Flares encased in metal cannisters, with internal triggering mechanisms, are far superior to the old-fashioned highway type in cardboard cases that must

Floating in a PFD or immersion suit, you present just 2 to 4 square feet of surface area to rescue units. You've got to make yourself bigger, brighter or different to have much chance of being found.

be struck for ignition.

Pyrotechnics should be used only when there is a good prospect of their being seen. Hand flares should be used only when you can hear or see a boat or plane. Rocket-propelled parachute flares and meteors can be seen over greater distances, depending upon the intensity and duration of burn and the atmospheric conditions, but they should be used only when you have reason to believe there may be a rescue unit within range.

Pyrotechnic devices should be treated as firearms and launched carefully to prevent injuries or damage to the raft. Hold flares downwind, at arm's length, and look away. Highway-type flares drip hot ash and wax. Don't let the hot material burn you or damage the raft. Metal cannister flares don't drip, but the cannisters get white hot. Be sure to hold the insulated handle and be extremely careful with the glowing cannister.

In strong winds, aim a parachute rocket or meteor at a 45-degree angle into the wind so that the signal is carried over your position. Don't aim a rocket-propelled flare or meteor at a rescue unit that is close at hand. A high-intensity parachute rocket reaches an altitude of 1,200 feet and burns for up to a minute. The helicopter pilot doesn't need that in the cockpit.

Depending on atmospheric conditions, parachute rockets are visible at distances up to 40 miles. In contrast, pistol-fired meteors reach a few hundred feet in altitude and burn for 4-6 seconds. Their visible ranges are much less. Be sure you know what you're buying.

High-intensity parachute rockets burn at 40,000 candlepower for up to a minute. They can be seen for more than 40 miles in clear visibility.

Orange smoke signals carried on the bridge or working deck provide excellent man-overboard signaling devices. There are also day/night man-overboard signals that incorporate signal lights and orange smoke, and can be attached to ring buoys.

Daylight Signals

Mirrors are the brightest daytime signals and can be fabricated out of any reflective surface. To use a mirror, focus the point of reflected light on your hand, then move your hand until it covers the place where you want to aim. Remove your hand and wiggle the mirror in all directions.

Any kind of light is a signal, but high-intensity strobes are the best. Attach a high-intensity strobe high on your PFD or immersion suit. The best places to have it would be as high as possible on the shoulder-front, or on the hood. Additionally, at least one of your ring buoys or throwable devices should be fitted with a signal light and heaving line.

Dyes and distress flags make you different. So does noise. You can blow a whistle longer and louder than you can yell, and a canned air horn is louder yet. If you are floating in calm water, splashing is a better means of making yourself bigger and different than waving. You've got to decide what signal is most effective depending on your circumstances.

A row of three fires or smoke pits on a beach definitely tells a pilot you're in trouble and not just camping. If you can't start a fire, pile debris in a highly unnatural shape like a letter or a triangle.

Keep the bigger, brighter, different philosophy in mind and use any means available to attract attention.

▪ Personal Survival Kits ▪

C oast Guard approved life rafts carry inventories of basic survival equipment, and you should be familiar with the contents of your vessel's raft. You can give yourself an extra margin of hope by assembling a Personal Survival Kit and stowing it with your immersion suit.

Your kit should be stowed in a water-repellent bag like those used by kayakers, and the bag should be fitted with a lanyard that can be used to attach the kit to the life raft or to your immersion suit.

Suggested contents are a wool watch cap, reflective space blanket, and plastic garbage bags that can be used to provide extra shelter.

A personal EPIRB, flares, a strobe light, a flashlight, a whistle and a signaling mirror are examples of signaling devices that can be stowed in the Personal Survival Kit.

Fresh water and a collapsible water container for adding to your water supply would be excellent additions, as would an emergency food supply, any prescription medicines you require, and a first-aid kit.

A folding knife, a length of cord, heavy-duty aluminum foil, and a fishing kit may prove extremely useful, and if you reach the shore, you may want to have waterproof matches or a lighter, along with fire starters and candles.

If you wear glasses or contacts, you may want to add a spare pair to the kit, and you should consider including a survival manual in case you become involved in an extended survival experience.

You must be the judge of what you need, based on where and how your vessel operates, your physical condition and the philosophy of the Seven Steps.

▪ Man Overboard ▪

There is one rule that guarantees your chances of surviving a man-overboard accident: don't be the man in the water. Even a few minutes of exposure to very cold water can be disabling to a crewman who lacks flotation *and* thermal protection.

Speed is the key to saving the crewman who does fall overboard. The skipper and remaining crew must function efficiently in a man-overboard emergency, and the man in the water must take whatever actions he can to minimize heat loss.

Saving a man overboard takes fast action by the entire crew. You'll probably make mistakes if your crew doesn't have pre-assigned duties that have been practiced in advance.

Man in the Water

If you're the man in the water, you've got to minimize heat loss at all costs. This can best be accomplished by getting the critical heat loss areas, especially the head and neck, out of the water.

If there is any source of buoyancy available, use it to get as much of your body as possible out of the water. Water robs body heat up to 25 times as fast as air of the same temperature.

If you are wearing a PFD with enough buoyancy to keep your head and neck out of the water, don't swim if help is close at hand. Assume the Heat Escape Lessening Posture, or HELP position, and let the boat come to you.

Remain calm and try to conserve your energy. Use whatever means are available to signal the vessel.

Action by the Crew

The crewmen who remain on deck when a man is lost overboard must do several things simultaneously. Coordination is vital.

1) Sound the Alarm. The skipper or helmsman must be advised immediately that there is a man over the side.

2) Throw a ring buoy, or some other form of flotation, together with a line. Try to retrieve the victim before he is out of heaving range.

3) Throw signals to mark the man's position. In darkness, throw a water light. In daylight, throw an orange smoke.

One man should serve as the "eyes" and do nothing but keep the victim in sight.

Never send a rescue swimmer into the water without an immersion suit and lifeline.

4) Keep the victim in sight. One man must serve as the eyes and assume no duties that interfere with his ability to watch the man or the last point at which he was observed.

5) Retrieve outlying gear that may interfere with maneuvering the vessel. If it cannot be quickly retrieved, cut it free.

6) Prepare a means of pick-up. One man should don an immersion suit in case the victim requires assistance in the water. The rescuer must be attached to a safety line before he goes over the side. Utilize a skiff or small boat if it can be quickly launched and sea conditions permit. Prepare a lifting appliance. An unconscious or helpless victim will be extremely difficult to lift over the rail.

Action by the Skipper or Helmsman

The skipper or helmsman must also perform multiple tasks in quick succession.

1) Record the accident site as a Loran C waypoint if your unit has a "Here" key that enables you to do it instantly.

2) Alert nearby vessels by radio.

3) Return to the spot by the fastest possible means. Marine texts describe four common recovery methods: the Anderson or One-turn, the Williamson Turn, the Race Track Turn, and Y-backing. You must use whatever method suits your vessel, the sea conditions and your gear style.

4) Form a lee, beam to the wind, with the vessel upwind of the victim.

5) Use full rudder to swing the stern away from the man. Keep him well forward of the propellers.

6) Take all way off. If possible, stop the shaft before the man reaches the vicinity of the stern.

7) After the recovery, treat the victim for hypothermia until his body core temperature returns to normal. He may argue that he is fine and requires no treatment, but treat him anyway. If he's severely hypothermic, or if you are unsure of his condition, call the Coast Guard and request medical advice or assistance. Treatment tips are offered in Chapter 14.

▪ Search and Rescue ▪

All vessels are morally obligated to respond to distress calls when they're in a position to provide search and rescue assistance. Depending on the circumstances, you could be called upon to respond to an emergency either independently, or in conjunction with specialized search and rescue units like the Coast Guard.

Coordination and communication are vital. If you're called upon to render assistance, you should maintain a continuous listening watch on the distress fre-

A Coast Guard 41-foot utility boat.

quency. You may be called upon to relay information to and from the Coast Guard, and you should advise the Coast Guard about your position and your estimated time of arrival on the scene. Normally, if you find yourself on the scene in conjunction with a Coast Guard unit, it will assume the role of on-scene commander, and you should follow instructions until you're released from your duty to assist.

There's an international signal for an aircraft that wants you to follow it to the scene of an emergency. The pilot will circle your vessel while opening and closing his throttle or changing the pitch of his propellers. He'll then cross close ahead of your vessel and proceed in the direction of the vessel in distress.

You should attempt to contact the aircraft on Channels 16 or 2182. If you can't make contact and your assistance is no longer needed, the pilot will cross your wake and repeat the signaling maneuver.

On your way to the scene, you may need to make special preparations such as fixing a means of retrieving survivors from the water. You should make use of radar in searching for the casualty, as well as any radio direction-finding equipment capable of locating transmissions from an EPIRB on 121.5 MHz or VHF channels 15 and 16. You should use lights, smoke or whistle signals to make yourself highly visible to survivors, and should post lookouts capable of searching in a 360-degree arc around your vessel.

You should be prepared to treat survivors for medical problems including hypothermia.

Assistance by Search and Rescue Aircraft

Vessels in distress may be supplied with equipment dropped by search and rescue aircraft. Possibilities are buoyant equipment cannisters, life rafts, radio beacons or transceivers, dye or smoke markers, parachute flares and salvage pumps.

Helicopters may be used to supply equipment or evacuate personnel. Keep in mind that helicopters have limited ranges, from 50 to 300 nautical

Helicopters can be used to supply equipment and evacuate personnel. This HH52 aircraft has been the Coast Guard standard but is now being phased out in favor of the H65 Dauphin.

In this drill, equipment is transferred in a rescue basket.

miles, and that rescue operations often place the flight crews in danger. Under no circumstances should a vessel request a helicopter evacuation unless it is faced with a serious emergency.

If you're in doubt about whether a helicopter evacuation is warranted, contact the Coast Guard, describe your situation and let them determine the best means of assistance. There may be a nearby vessel with a doctor aboard, or some other source of help unknown to you.

In supplying equipment, a helicopter normally hovers over a cleared space on deck and lowers the gear with its winch cable. All you have to do is unhook the cable.

For personnel evacuation, a helicopter may lower a member of its own crew to assist with the rescue. The end of the hoisting cable may be outfitted with one of the following devices:

Coast Guard personnel practice a water hoist in Puget Sound.

A rescue sling is put on like a coat. Face the hook and make sure the loop passes behind your back and under both armpits. Clasp your hands in front. Don't sit on the sling, or unhook it from the cable.

A rescue basket doesn't require any special procedures. Simply climb in, remain seated and hold on.

A rescue net resembles a bird cage open on two sides. Like the rescue basket, all you have to do is climb in, remain seated and hold on.

A rescue seat looks like an anchor with flat prongs or seats. To use it, simply sit on the prongs and wrap your arms around the shank. You may have to fold down the prongs prior to mounting.

Injury victims will be lifted in a rescue litter provided by the helicopter. You'll have to transfer the victim to the rescue litter even if you've already placed him on a backboard or stretcher. You should move the victim as gently as possible, especially if you suspect back or neck injuries.

An injury victim should be tagged to indicate his condition, any medication that's been given to him, and when it was given.

If you have to move the litter away from the hoist area to load the victim, unhook it from the cable and leave the cable free for the helicopter to hoist in again. *Never* attach the cable to your vessel. Be sure the victim is securely strapped into the litter.

Action Aboard the Vessel

Make sure your crewmen are wearing PFDs or immersion suits.

Mark your position with signals. At night, use deck lights or search lights, but never shine a light directly at the helicopter. You might blind the pilot. Use flares, smokes and dyes when you're confident that someone can see them.

Try to establish direct radio contact with the helicopter on Channels 16 or 2182. The pilot needs information on your position, your course and speed, and prevailing weather conditions prior to his arrival at the scene. Once he is on-scene, you should follow his instructions.

If you don't have radio contact, use the following hoisting signals:

Do Not Hoist: Arms extended horizontally, fingers clenched, thumbs down.

Hoist: Arms raised above the horizontal, thumbs up.

The noise of the helicopter may make it impossible to communicate verbally on deck. You should devise a set of hand signals for use among your crew.

Clear a section of the deck as a pickup area. Make sure it's clear of rigging, booms, wires and loose gear. Light the pickup area as well as possible during a night rescue. Be prepared to move the pickup area, or to alter your course and speed, if the pilot instructs you to.

Allow a metal part of the lifting device to touch the deck to eliminate the static electric shock hazard before any member of the crew touches the lifting device. If there's a trail line attached to the lifting device, use it to guide the basket or litter to the deck. The trail line won't cause a shock.

▪ Hypothermia ▪

H ypothermia is the lowering of body core temperature because of exposure to a cold environment. If the exposure is prolonged, the core temperature reaches a level from which the body can no longer rewarm itself. At that point, unless the victim receives effective first aid, he or she will die. Hypothermia is a special danger at sea, because exposure to cold water causes heat loss much faster than exposure to cold air.

Even a few minutes of exposure to very cold water can produce hypothermia, and you should treat for it even if the victim of a man-overboard accident or a capsized skiff says he feels fine. Like a drunk, a hypothermia victim is the worst judge of his own condition.

The shock of sudden immersion in cold water can cause circulatory problems that may not appear immediately, and a crewman who has just been pulled over the side isn't out of danger until his core temperature has returned to near normal. If his core temperature is less than 95 degrees F., he needs treatment, and if it's less than 90 degrees F., he's in serious trouble.

The normal, household thermometer only reads to the level where hypothermia begins, so you need a rectal hypothermic thermometer to do a good job of diagnosing a cold-related condition like hypothermia, and to get accurate medical advice on how to treat it.

Treatment may range from simply sending the man to his bunk briefly in a mild case, to calling for a medical evacuation, performing CPR and striving to actively rewarm a severely hypothermic patient. A number of treatment techniques are standard no matter how serious the injury. It is the issue of rewarming that causes most of the confusion related to hypothermia.

Rewarm Slowly

Keep in mind that the victim has to be rewarmed slowly. Rewarming him too fast, by putting him in a hot shower, for example, could kill him. And, rewarm his body core—his head, neck and torso—not his arms and legs. Once the core begins to rewarm, it will take care of the arms and legs by circulating warm blood toward the extremities. On the other hand, rewarming the arms and legs won't help the important region, the core. In fact, rewarming the arms and legs first will make the core get colder, as we'll see in a minute.

The first step in all cases is to get the victim out of the cold environment. If he's been in cold water more than a few minutes, he will probably be unable to help himself so you'll have to go and get him. If you have to enter the water to rescue him, be sure you're wearing an immersion suit and safety line. Protecting yourself is the first rule of first aid.

Another important consideration is to handle him as gently as you can. The shock of exposure to cold water puts the circulatory system under stress, and rough handling could cause a heart attack or other circulatory problems.

Insulate Underneath

If you have enough help, carry him in a horizontal position, get him someplace warm and lay him on his back. On many vessels, this probably means the galley floor. You have access to supplies in the galley, you want the environment where you treat him to be room temperature, no hotter, and you don't want to carry him any farther than you have to. If you use the floor or some other cold surface, be sure to insulate the victim underneath with blankets or some other form of covering.

Check the ABCs (airway, breathing and circulation) immediately. You may have to breathe for him and perform chest compressions. Hypothermia victims may appear dead when there is still life in the body core. If you begin CPR, don't stop until the victim has been rewarmed. You can't be sure a victim of cold-related injury is dead until he's warm and dead. Techniques for checking the ABCs and performing CPR are covered in standard first-aid courses and texts.

Gently remove his wet clothing and wrap him in something warm and dry. If possible, use a hypothermic wrap in which you wrap his torso in one set of blankets or coverings, then wrap each arm and leg separately. The object is to isolate his body core so you can rewarm it separately from his extremities. If you don't have enough material for a hypothermic wrap, use dry clothes, a sleeping bag or even a plastic garbage bag—anything that helps keep him from getting any colder.

Put a watch cap on his head. The head is the source of more than half the body's heat loss.

If he's mildly hypothermic, he'll be cold but conscious and reasonably alert. Keep him quiet even if he protests and says he's alright. Don't give him hot drinks unless he's *clearly* able to swallow, and never give him any alcohol. Don't rub or manipulate his arms and legs. Never put him in a hot shower.

You have to keep him quiet and lying flat to stabilize his heart rate and minimize the danger of circulatory problems, and you want his body core to slowly rewarm itself. Don't rewarm his arms and legs. The core will take care of that. Just insulate the arms and legs so he's not losing more heat through the extremities.

To help his body rewarm itself, use objects that are warm, not hot, and apply them to the head, neck, chest or groin. Good choices are hot pads or hot water bottles, chemical "heat packs", or objects you have warmed in the oven, like rocks or even potatoes. Touch them to your own skin first to be sure they're not too hot. The patient won't be able to tell if you're burning him.

An excellent technique for gentle rewarming is body-to-body contact. Take off your shirt, exercise for a moment to raise your own body temperature, get under the coverings and press your torso next to his. Stay there until it's obvious he's getting warmer.

Keep him on his back until you're sure his temperature is rising. When he's stopped shivering, is fully conscious and clearly able to swallow, and is obviously nearly warm again, you can give him warm fluids, but keep him quiet and continue to watch him. A hypothermia victim who recovers should have no lasting effects from the incident, but circulatory problems like heart attacks are possible until his body has returned to normal.

If he has any of the following symptoms, he's severely hypothermic and you should seek professional advice.

■ Depressed vital signs.

■ Unconsciousness or semi-consciousness and an inability to walk, speak or think normally.

■ A core temperature of 90 degrees F. or less.

■ An inability to shiver despite being very cold. Shivering is a good sign and means that the body is still trying to rewarm itself. A victim too cold to shiver is in trouble, although someone who has been drinking may not shiver at all.

Why is Gentle Rewarming so Important?

The body acts like a thermostat as it strives to regulate its own core temperature at a constant level of about 98.6 degrees F. The core consists of the head, neck and torso where the vital organs are housed, and while the arms and legs can be subject to large fluctuations in temperature without any threat to life, the core can tolerate temperature shifts of only a few degrees.

Just as a fever that causes a rise in core temperature of more than a few degrees means that you're very sick, a core temperature drop to less than about 95 degrees F. means that you're entering the danger zone.

An obvious body reaction to rising temperatures is perspiration, which causes evaporative cooling of the skin. Shivering is an equally obvious reaction to falling temperatures, as the body utilizes muscle activity to try and rewarm itself.

Not so obvious is the way circulation is affected by exposure to cold. The body core is vital for life. The arms and legs are not. As the body cools, life retreats from the extremities toward the core as the brain shuts down blood flow to the arms and legs in an attempt to minimize heat loss around the vital organs.

Last Line of Defense

By restricting blood flow to the extremities where it would be rapidly cooled, the body forms a last line of defense around the core. If exposure to the cold continues, even this defense eventually fails.

If the body is returned to a warm environment soon enough, however, life can be sustained in the core even if the victim shows no outward signs of life. As long as the core temperature hasn't fallen too far, the body can recover and life will be gradually restored to the extremities.

Active rewarming with dry, gentle sources of warmth applied to the core aids the recovery process.

The danger in rewarming too rapidly, or in rewarming the arms and legs first, occurs because a hypothermia victim's extremities are full of cold blood. Sudden rewarming sends a signal to the brain that the cold emergency is over. At that point, the brain may reopen circulation to the extremities too fast, and the result is a sudden return of cold blood to the body core. This "after drop" in core temperature may be the additional stress that the patient's heart and circulatory system can't endure.

In the case of hypothermia, or any medical emergency, contact the Coast Guard and seek professional advice. If you can provide good information about the victim's condition—things like core temperature and vital signs—the Coast Guard can quickly obtain professional medical advice to help guide your treatment efforts.

▪ Float Plan ▪

Voyage and Vessel Information

Date info furnished _____   Type & Name of vessel _____

Planned Itinerary

Depart _____ at _____ for _____ ETA _____

Enroute or Alternate Ports _____ ETA _____ ETD _____

_____ ETA _____ ETD _____

_____ ETA _____ ETD _____

Misc. Info: _____

Purpose of trip _____

Vessel Description

Official Number: _____ Homeport: _____ Length: _____

Beam: _____ Draft: _____ Freeboard: _____

Type of rig: _____ Any hull markings: _____

Colors: Hull: _____ Superstructure: _____ Deck: _____

Owner: _____

Built by: _____ Year: _____ Hull Material: _____

Prominent features: Bowsprit _____ Fish Pulpit _____ Fly Bridge _____

Boat Stowage _____ Other _____

Photo attached: _____

Survival Equipment

Food and water on vessel (in days): _____

Boat: Type _____ Material _____ Length _____

Capacity _____ Color _____ Markings _____

Raft: Type _____ Material _____ How stowed _____

Capacity _____ Color _____ Markings _____

Portable radio: Transmitter? _____ Freqs _____ Signal _____

Auto? _____

Receiver? _____ Remarks _____

continues

EPIRB: Yes / No, Class? (A), (B) or (C), Where stowed? _____

Emergency gear: Flares? _____   Smoke? _____   Mirror? _____

                   Radar? _____   Reflector? _____   Dye? _____

                   Water? _____   Rations? _____   Lights? _____

                   Other? _____

Number, type, color, markings of lifejackets, survival suits, rings, and other flotation gear: _____

_____

_____

Personnel

Operator's qualifications and experience: _____

_____

Number of persons on board: _____

Data on persons on board:

Name	Address	Age	Sex	Citizenship

Remarks

Use the space to record any other desired info: _____

_____

_____

_____

Communications

Frequencies available _____ Call sign _____

Transmitter power _____ Aux Gen _____ Batteries _____

Communications schedule: Will contact: _____

       on Freq. _____ at _____ .

Will contact _____ on Freq. _____ at _____

Will contact _____ on Freq. _____ at _____

Will contact _____ on Freq. _____ at _____

Names and address of points of contact:

At point of departure: _____

At destination: _____

Others: _____

To whom & by what means will arrival be reported _____

Navigation and Propulsion

Compass? _____ Condition _____ Sextant? _____ Proficiency _____

Radio direction finder? _____Freq. _____ Range _____

Calibrated? _____ Loran? _____ Radar? _____ Fathometer? _____

Number, type & HP of engines _____

Cruising Speed _____ Range _____ Fuel Capacity _____

If sail, estimated speed under various wind conditions: _____

If sail, type rig _____

Spare sails _____If auxiliary, when is engine used?

Search and Rescue Units

The following people and organizations should be notified as soon as there is reason to believe (because of the lack of communication with or non-appearance of this vessel or any other incident) that the vessel may have been lost or imperiled.

Name _____ Phone number _____

US COAST GUARD _____

_____

_____

_____

▪ Distress Communications ▪

(Post near your radio telephone)

Instructions: Complete this form now (except for items 6 through 9)

SPEAK SLOWLY—CLEARLY—CALMLY
1. Make sure your radiotelephone is on.

2. Select either *VHF Channel 16* (156.8 MHz) OR *2182* kHz.

3. Press microphone button and say: "MAYDAY—MAYDAY—MAYDAY."

4. Say: "THIS IS_____ _____ _____

           your boat name   your boat name   your boat name

                                 your call letters

5. Say: "MAYDAY: _____

                             your boat name

6. TELL WHERE YOU ARE: Loran, Latitude and Longitude or reference to landmark.

7. STATE THE NATURE OF YOUR DISTRESS.

8. GIVE NUMBER OF ADULTS AND CHILDREN ABOARD, AND CONDITIONS OF ANY INJURED.

9. ESTIMATE PRESENT SEAWORTHINESS OF YOUR BOAT.

10. BRIEFLY DESCRIBE YOUR BOAT:

_____ ; _____ FEET;

    Registration No.   Length

_____FEET; _____, _____HULL; _____TRIM;

 Draft   Type   Color   Color

_____MASTS; _____POWER; _____

 Number   Type; Horsepower   Construction Material

Anything else you think will help rescuers to find you

11. Say: "I WILL BE LISTENING ON CHANNEL *16/2182*."
(Cross out channel no. or frequency that does not apply)

12. End Message by saying: "THIS IS _____ . OVER."

                  your boat name and call sign

13. Release microphone button and listen: Someone should answer. IF THEY DO NOT, REPEAT CALL, BEGINNING AT ITEM 3.
If there is still no answer, switch to another channel and begin again.

FORM D-30-A REV. 7/84

STATION BILL
SIGNALS

FIRE AND EMERGENCY .... One continuous blast of the Ship's Whistle and continuous ringing of General Alarm Bells, simultaneously sounded for not less than 10 seconds.

ABANDON SHIP .... 7 Short Blasts and 1 Long Blast of the Whistle and the same signal on the General Alarm Bells.

MAN OVERBOARD .... Hail, and pass the word MAN OVERBOARD to the Bridge. Sound the letter "O" (- - -) several (at least 4) times on the ships whistle followed by the same signal on the general alarm.

DISMISSAL .... From FIRE AND EMERGENCY stations, 3 Short Blasts on the Whistle and 3 Short Rings on the General Alarm Bells.

GENERAL INSTRUCTIONS

1) Each person, upon boarding the vessel, shall familiarize himself with his assigned location, in the event of an emergency.
2) All crew members shall be thoroughly familiar with the duties they are assigned to perform in the event of an emergency.
3) Each person on board shall participate in emergency drills and shall be properly dressed, including a properly donned life preserver.
4) All persons, in addition to crew, shall participate in emergency drills, assisting as directed by either the Chief Mate or Chief Engineer, depending on the area in which they are working.
5) The Chief Mate shall be responsible for the maintenance and readiness of all lifesaving and firefighting appliances and equipment in and around the house, the main deck, and pumproom.
6) The Chief Engineer shall be responsible for the maintenance and readiness of all lifesaving and firefighting appliances and equipment within the engine room spaces and steering gear room.
7) The Chief Mate is in overall charge of the emergency squads if the emergency is outside the engine spaces. The First Assistant Engineer is in overall charge of the emergency squads if the emergency is in the engine spaces.

WHERE WHISTLE SIGNALS ARE USED FOR HANDLING BOATS

LOWER BOATS .... 1 SHORT BLAST ON WHISTLE
STOP LOWERING BOATS .... 2 SHORT BLASTS ON WHISTLE
DISMISSAL FROM BOAT STATIONS .... 3 SHORT BLASTS ON WHISTLE

FIRE AND EMERGENCY INSTRUCTIONS

1) Any person discovering a fire shall notify the bridge by sounding the nearest available alarm and then take any initial actions needed, fighting the fire with available equipment.
2) Upon nearing the fire and emergency signal all air ports, watertight doors, fire doors, scuppers and designated discharges shall be closed and all fans, blowers and ventilating systems shall be stopped. Personnel assigned to these duties shall check to ensure this item is completed.
3) Immediately upon hearing the Fire and Emergency Signal fire pumps are to be started and if appropriate fire hoses led out to the affected area.
4) Upon seeing a "Man Overboard" immediately throw a life ring (with a light attached if at night) and notify the bridge by reporting "Man Overboard Port (Starboard) Side." In all cases keep the man in sight.
The officer on watch, with due regard to safety of navigation, should initiate a Williamson turn. All available hands should be put on lookout with at least one man aloft. The Emergency Boat Crew, consisting of all lifeboatmen, shall immediately clear the lee boat for launching. Steward department personnel are to provide blankets at the lifeboat and then prepare the hospital for treating possible cases of exposure.

5) Helmsman and OMU or QMED on watch remain on watch.

Form by J.P. Grundy Printers, Inc. 11 Dixon Avenue, Copaique, NY 11726

ABANDON SHIP-BOAT STATIONS

FIRE AND EMERGENCY STATIONS

STBD EMERGENCY SQUAD ( )

NO.	RATING				BOAT NO. OR LIFERAFT

PORT EMERGENCY SQUAD ( )

NO.	RATING				BOAT NO. OR LIFERAFT

MASTER

• About the Publisher •

John Sabella & Associates Inc., is a firm that specializes in developing information, education and communications programs for business and industry.

The firm consults with vessel owners, industry associations, insurance companies and other organizations from around the country on marine safety issues, and regularly presents training seminars on sea safety and survival.

Working in conjunction with The North Pacific Fishing Vessel Owners' Association, the U.S. Coast Guard and the National Marine Fisheries Service, John Sabella & Associates Inc., developed the following programs for the commercial fishing industry:

> *The Vessel Safety Manual* A comprehensive work that represents the operational component of the Voluntary Safety Standards for U.S. commercial fishing vessels.
>
> *The Crew Training Program*, offering hands-on instruction in:
> Safety Equipment & Survival Procedures
> Fire Prevention & Control
> Medical Emergencies at Sea
> Navigation & Stability
>
> *The Safety & Survival at Sea Videotape Series*, broadcast-quality training aids with the following titles:
> Safety Equipment & Survival Procedures
> Fire Prevention & Control
> Medical Emergencies at Sea
> Fishing Vessel Stability

Other Recent Publications:

> *Coping with Casualties at Sea: The Role of Ownership & Management*

Other Recent Video Titles:

> *Harvesting Distant Waters: Seattle's Dynamic Fishing Fleet*

▪ Notes ▪